AL CAPONE SHINES MY SHOES

by
Gennifer Choldenko

Teacher Guide

Written by
Monica L. Odle

> **Note**
> The 2009 Dial Books for Young Readers hardcover edition, © 2009 by Gennifer Choldenko, was used to prepare this guide. The page references may differ in other editions. Novel ISBN: 978-0-8037-3460-9
>
> **Please note:** Please assess the appropriateness of this book for the age level and maturity of your students prior to reading and discussing it with them.

ISBN 978-1-56137-990-3

Copyright infringement is a violation of Fe...

© 2010 by Novel Units, Inc., Bulverde, Texas. All rights...
be reproduced, translated, stored in a retrieval system, o...
(electronic, mechanical, photocopying, recording, or oth...
from ECS Learning Systems, Inc.

Photocopying of student worksheets by a classroom teacher at a non-profit school who has purchased this publication for his/her own class is permissible. Reproduction of any part of this publication for an entire school or for a school system, by for-profit institutions and tutoring centers, or for commercial sale is strictly prohibited.

Novel Units is a registered trademark of ECS Learning Systems, Inc.
Printed in the United States of America.

Table of Contents

Summary 3

About the Author 3

Characters 4

Background Information 5

Initiating Activities 6

Vocabulary Activities 6

Seven Sections 7
  Each section contains: Summary, Vocabulary,
  Discussion Questions, and Supplementary Activities

Post-reading Discussion Questions 21

Post-reading Extension Activities 24

Assessment 25

Scoring Rubric 31

Skills and Strategies

Thinking
  Research, brainstorming, decision-making, inferring, compare/contrast

Comprehension
  Predicting, summarizing, sequencing

Writing
  Poetry, journal, report, newspaper article, summary, letter, outline

Listening/Speaking
  Oral presentation, discussion, interview

Vocabulary
  Definitions, parts of speech, synonyms/antonyms

Literary Elements
  Setting, point of view, conflict, theme, characterization, figurative language, foreshadowing

Across the Curriculum
  Art—poster, caricature, diorama; History—Alcatraz, baseball, J. Edgar Hoover, vaudeville, Great Depression, technology; Health—CPR, autism; Science—scientific process, geography; Math—budget, wages

Genre: historical fiction

Setting: Alcatraz Island; 1935

Point of View: first person

Themes: integrity, trust, family, friendship, empathy, responsibility, solidarity

Conflict: person vs. person, person vs. self, person vs. society, person vs. nature

Tone: honest, informal, humorous

Summary

Twelve-year-old Moose Flanagan lives on Alcatraz, where his father works as a guard and electrician. Life on Alcatraz is complicated for Moose, as his quietly magnetic personality draws many different kinds of people to him. Throughout the story, Moose struggles to balance the various friendships in his life with his duties as a responsible son, brother, and Alcatraz resident. However, these challenges are made all the more difficult by Moose's interactions with the island's convicts. Al Capone, who helped get Moose's autistic sister, Natalie, into the Esther P. Marinoff School, is expecting a favor from Moose. In addition, some of the convicts are hatching an escape plan, which Moose and his friends must try to foil without getting their fathers fired. Friendships and character are tested, and in the end, Moose and his friends and family realize themselves as essential parts of a vast support system keeping the island, and each other, afloat.

About the Author

Gennifer Choldenko was born in Santa Monica, California in 1957 and is the youngest of four children. She knew she wanted to be a writer at age six and credits her father with inspiring this decision. After graduating from Brandeis University with a degree in literature and creative writing, she worked as a copywriter for a large advertising agency. Though Choldenko loved her job, she decided to pursue a profession she would enjoy even more—writing and illustrating. Her earlier books include *Notes From a Liar and Her Dog* and *Moonstruck: The True Story of the Cow Who Jumped Over the Moon*. *Al Capone Does My Shirts* won the Newbery Honor award in 2005. *How to Make Friends with a Giant, Louder, Lili, If a Tree Falls at Lunch Period*, and *Al Capone Shines My Shoes* followed. Upon its release, the latter was named by *Kirkus Reviews*, Barnes & Noble, and the *San Francisco Chronicle* as one of the Best Children's Books of 2009. Choldenko researches her stories' subject matter thoroughly before writing but says she relies as much on her intuition as her intellect. She lives in the San Francisco Bay area with her husband and two children. Choldenko's advice to young writers is to "write about what you want desperately to understand" (source: http://www.choldenko.com; Web site active at time of publication).

Characters

Matthew "Moose" Flanagan: affable 12-year-old boy who lives on Alcatraz with his family; loves baseball and his family; has a crush on Piper

Natalie Flanagan: Moose's 16-year-old sister; autistic; gifted at math; attends the Esther P. Marinoff School

Helen Flanagan: Natalie and Moose's mother; piano teacher; devoted to her children while expecting much from them

Cam Flanagan: Natalie and Moose's father; electrician and prison guard on Alcatraz; defined by his warmth and integrity

Theresa Mattaman: gregarious seven-year-old girl who lives on Alcatraz; one of Natalie's favorite people

Jimmy Mattaman: Theresa's 12-year-old brother; sensitive; prefers doing experiments to playing baseball

Rocky Mattaman: Theresa and Jimmy's infant brother

Anna Maria Mattaman: Theresa, Jimmy, and Rocky's mother; compassionate; makes wonderful cannolis

Riv Mattaman: Theresa, Jimmy, and Rocky's father and Anna Maria's husband; forgiving; guard who often works the tower

Annie Bomini: 12-year-old girl who lives on the island; good at baseball; has a crush on Moose and strong moral convictions

Mrs. Bomini: Annie's mother; talkative, adores Moose; mistakenly thinks Moose loves needlepoint as much as she does

Scout McIlvey: Moose's school friend who loves baseball; fun-loving but self-centered

Piper Williams: the warden's daughter; beautiful but hot-tempered and prone to mischief; secretly insecure; has a crush on Moose

Warden Williams: Alcatraz's warden; desperately wants his pregnant wife to bear a son; enjoys getting free labor from skilled convicts

June Williams: Piper's mother and the warden's wife; kind; pregnant and very ill

Officer Darby Trixle: Alcatraz guard; detached and self-important; likes to make life difficult for convicts as well as some officers and their families

Bea Trixle: Darby's wife; runs the island's canteen; wishes her husband were more thoughtful

Janet Trixle: Darby and Bea's seven-year-old daughter; follows her father's lead and is a stickler for rules

Mrs. Caconi: older woman at whose apartment the women gather to talk privately; helps look after the warden's new baby while June is in the hospital

Al Capone (AZ 85): notorious prisoner at Alcatraz; charismatic; helped Natalie get into the Marinoff School and requests a favor of Moose in return

Buddy Boy: convicted con man; performs various housekeeping tasks in the Williams home; loves to entertain and is a talented actor

Willy One Arm: convicted thief; helps prepare food in the Williams home; has his pet mouse, Molly, with him at all times

Seven Fingers: convicted ax murderer; often fixes the plumbing in the building where the Flanagans live

AZ 105: convict on gardening detail who befriended Natalie before she left for school and he was released

Background Information

The following information will enhance students' understanding of the novel.

1. Autism is a condition that generally affects one's ability to communicate in socially acceptable ways. The brain and sensory system of autistic people work together differently than in non-autistics. The story is set in the 1930s, when the term "autism" had yet to be coined. At this time, many people with the condition were misunderstood and sent to institutions or were subject to experimental treatment. Autistic individuals generally take longer to learn how to use language and nonverbal cues, and many autistic people say that they find it easier to express themselves through writing or typing. Some also experience dulled or very heightened sensory perception. An overload of sensory perception makes some autistic people prone to uncontrollable outbursts that may last minutes, hours, or days. Autistic people tend to prefer schedules and routine since predictability lessens the chances of sensory overload. About 10% of people with autism are exceptionally gifted in mathematics, art, or music. Some members of the autistic community view their condition as a disorder and are interested in finding a cure for autism. However, other autistic people view autism as merely a unique way of life and have no desire for a cure.

2. Alcatraz served as the United States' foremost federal penitentiary for the country's worst criminals for 29 years from 1934–1963. It is a 12-acre island in the San Francisco Bay. It is true that people who worked on the island also lived there, and it is also true that the warden's home was very close to the cell blocks. The prison was eventually closed due to the fact that the facility was in disrepair, and it took a great deal of money to keep the system running. The Native-American population claimed the island for a short time after the prison closed, but with few natural resources available, their community became unstable and suffered many hardships. Eventually, the Native-American population released their claim on the island, and "The Rock" became a major tourist attraction. The author outlines which parts of her story are based on fact and which are fictional in the "Author's Note" at the end of the novel.

3. The Great Depression began when the stock market crashed on "Black Tuesday," October 29, 1929. In 1935, the setting for this novel, the country was still struggling to recover from this economic disaster. While unemployment rates did drop for a time after Franklin D. Roosevelt was elected President in 1932, they did not remain low. Understanding how difficult it was to find a job also adds weight to the children's fears of their fathers' dismissal should someone discover the bar spreader that Natalie brings onto the island.

Initiating Activities

1. Brainstorming: Using the Attribute Web on page 26 of this guide, allow students to brainstorm what they know about Alcatraz. Then have them conduct research to determine if what they know is fact or fiction.

2. History: Have students research significant events that happened or were happening in the United States in 1935. What books, movies, and music were popular? What kind of technology was prominent or new? Which sports or athletes were popular? Students should create a visual display to present their research.

3. Prediction: Instruct students to read the novel's Table of Contents and predict what the novel will be about based on the chapter titles.

4. Research: Divide students into groups, and have them conduct research on Al Capone. What did the public think of Al Capone? As they read the novel, have students compare and contrast what they know about the convict with the story's depiction of him. (Note: Teachers should oversee research relating to Al Capone's crimes.)

5. Writing: Have students write a poem or short story that describes a person's fear of telling the truth about something important. Students should consider why a person would lie or withhold the truth and what kind of inner struggle that person might be facing.

Vocabulary Activities

1. Vocabulary Squares: Select nine students to sit in three rows of three in the classroom. Give each student a large cutout of an X and an O. Then select two other students: one student is "X," and the other is "O." Student X is asked to define a vocabulary word. S/he must choose one of the nine students sitting in a square to define the word and then state whether s/he agrees or disagrees with the given definition. If Student X correctly agrees or disagrees with the given definition, the sitting student must display an X. If Student X incorrectly agrees or disagrees, the sitting student displays an O. Alternate turns between Students O and X. The first student to have three Xs or Os in a row (vertical, horizontal, or diagonal) is the winner.

2. Glossary: Ask students to keep a list of any unfamiliar or difficult words they encounter as they read the novel. Have students create a glossary from their lists. Glossaries should include each word's pronunciation, part of speech, and definition as it is used in the text.

3. Start/Stop: Divide the class into two teams. Have one person from each team stand at opposite ends of the room. Each team is given a vocabulary word at random, which it must be able to define without assistance. If a team is able to define the selected vocabulary word, its standing teammate may move forward one step. If a team answers incorrectly, the opposing team's standing member may move forward three steps. The team whose standing teammate reaches the opposite side of the room first wins.

4. Mix and Match: Write vocabulary words and their definitions separately on index cards. Make sure there are enough for each student to have one word and one definition card that do not match. Have students move around the room and attempt to match their words with others' definition cards. After all cards are paired, use a dictionary to see if the pairings are correct.

5. Sentence-by-Sentence: As a class, brainstorm a sentence to start a story. Then have students pass around a sheet of paper with the starter sentence at the top. Each student must add one sentence to the story which correctly uses a vocabulary word. After each student has contributed to the story, have a volunteer read the story aloud.

Chapters 1–4

Moose explains how Natalie was admitted into the Esther P. Marinoff School. Natalie leaves for school, and Moose and Jimmy visit their secret crawlspace beneath 64 building. Moose receives a new note from Al Capone that Annie inadvertently intercepts. Annie learns about Moose's involvement with Capone and insists that Moose tell what has happened. Moose refuses, and Annie in turn refuses to play baseball with him. Scout visits the island, and he and Moose meet the convicts working in the warden's house.

Vocabulary

civilians
menagerie
notorious
wheedles
starboard
gravitate
wary
pleading
carping
switchback

Discussion Questions

1. Where does the narrator live? What does he think of his living situation? *(He lives on Alcatraz Island. Answers will vary. Moose is both fascinated by and fearful of Alcatraz. Also, while he realizes that there are rules he must follow, he is frustrated with how Darby Trixle treats him.)*

2. What happens as the Flanagan family sends Natalie off to her new school? What do Officer Trixle's actions suggest about him, and what role do you think he will play in the story? *(The family takes care to keep Natalie calm, but Trixle orders the tower to shoot at the water even though Cam asked him not to and the only boat in sight is departing. Trixle then says that Natalie's reaction warrants an incident report. Answers will vary. Trixle knew there was no reason to shoot, and he also knew that the shots might upset Natalie. In addition, Trixle seems to delight in the possibility that Natalie might not return to Alcatraz. It is reasonable to say that Trixle enjoys feeling powerful, has something against Natalie, and will likely be an antagonist throughout the story.)*

3. Do you think Al Capone would do something nice without asking for anything in return? *(Answers will vary, but Capone's words, "Your turn," seem to indicate that he will soon require a favor of Moose.)*

4. What does Moose tell Annie? How does she react? Do you think it is good or bad that Annie knows Moose's secret? Explain. *(Moose tells Annie about his communications with Al Capone, and she is very alarmed at the possible consequences of Moose's behavior. She pressures him to tell someone about what is happening. Answers will vary.)*

5. Explain whether you think it is a good or bad idea for Buddy Boy and Willy One Arm to be working in the warden's house. *(Answers will vary. One view is that someone who breaks laws would probably have little respect for doing what is responsible and right and might be dangerous. On the other hand, working in the warden's house offers them special treatment they may not be willing to sacrifice by misbehaving.)*

6. What do you think of Scout's system of categorizing girls? Do you think it is right to attempt to categorize people? Is there a way to do so accurately? Explain. *(Answers will vary, but note that Scout's categories are subjective; Scout and Moose disagree on where Annie fits. Additionally, it is shallow to attempt to put all girls into one of three categories. People are diverse and unique and what makes them valuable often extends far beyond their appearances. Moose seems to realize this, as, in addition to defending Annie's looks, he points out Annie's talents as a baseball player.)*

7. Describe the relationships between some of the children in the novel—Moose, Annie, Scout, Piper, and Jimmy. *(Answers will vary. Moose and Jimmy are best friends on the island even though Jimmy is not a good baseball player, so Moose prefers to play ball with Scout, his friend from school. Scout realizes that Moose likes Piper but does not hesitate to tease him about it or flirt with Piper. Annie may be average-looking, but she is a responsible, honest friend and an excellent baseball player. She might have a crush on Moose but knows that Moose likes Piper.)*

8. **Prediction:** What will result from Moose's communications with Al Capone?

Supplementary Activities

1. Figurative Language: Begin a chart identifying the figurative language used in the novel. Continue adding to the chart as you read the novel. Examples: **Similes**—"convicts…as slippery as eels in axle grease" (p. 1); "spray of firepower that pounds like fireworks exploding inside your head" (p. 7); "…his face is pinched like his belt is a notch too tight" (p. 7); **Metaphors**—convicts: rotten fruit (p. 1); Mrs. Bomini: talking machine (p. 13); Al Capone's hit men: gorillas (p. 27)

2. Comprehension: Begin a character chart. As new characters are introduced, write down information about them. Add to the chart as you continue reading.

3. Writing: Moose describes the secret passageway he shares with Jimmy. In this passageway, they can tell each other anything. Write a poem that describes a place that is safe and protected where you feel free the way Moose feels in the passageway.

4. Math: Calculate how much it might cost to employ a personal cook for one month. Then calculate how much it might cost to have a personal housekeeper for one month. In today's world, approximately how much money do you think the warden would be saving by having two convicts work in his home?

Chapters 5–8

Scout and Moose find Jimmy while Theresa convinces Annie to join the baseball game. Jimmy plays poorly and distances himself from the others after Scout says he throws like a "dead girl." Annie, however, plays well enough to earn Scout's respect. Later that night, Moose talks with his dad about how to interact with the convicts and finds a note from Capone in his pillowcase, which he determines was left by Seven Fingers. The next morning, Moose finds he has developed hives. Mrs. Flanagan seems happy to take care of Moose and even apologizes to Moose for focusing on Natalie so much. Moose goes to the canteen to make amends with Jimmy. However, Rocky begins suffocating while playing with Theresa, and Moose must rush Rocky to Doc Ollie, who extracts a penny from Rocky's throat.

Discussion Questions

1. How does Scout treat Annie and Jimmy? What do you think of Scout? *(Scout patronizes Annie because she is a girl and assumes she will not be good at baseball. He mocks Jimmy's throw during the ball game, angering Jimmy and causing him to quit. Scout then calls for Theresa to take his place. Answers will vary, but Scout is quite disrespectful and seems only to value others in proportion to their playing ability.)*

Vocabulary
suspect
incredulously
bellows
methodically
contemplating
incentive
dredge
equator
averts
engorging
harness
cylinders
forceps
gullet
culprit

2. Moose's father says, "Treat a man like a dog, he'll act like a dog. Treat a man with respect, he'll remember that too. But trust [the criminals]? Not on your life" (p. 51). Do you agree or disagree with Cam's view of how to treat the convicts? Compare his opinion to that of the warden and Darby Trixle. With whom do you most agree? *(Answers will vary. The warden obviously trusts the cons far more than Cam does since he has two living in his home. Darby Trixle does not think the cons deserve any trust or respect.)*

3. What does the scene where Moose reveals he has hives tell readers about the Flanagans and especially Helen and Moose's relationship? *(Until now, Helen has not had as much time for Moose as she or he would have liked. With Natalie enrolled at the Marinoff School, the Flanagans finally feel that Natalie is getting the help she needs and can devote time and emotion to other things in their lives. However tentative they are about doing so, both Helen and Moose are taking the first steps to bridging the emotional gap that has formed between them.)*

4. How does Moose finally decide to do what Capone asks of him? Do you agree or disagree with his logic? What would you do if you were in Moose's place? *(While Moose fully comprehends the risks in getting [and not getting] Mae roses, his fears of Capone and getting caught are overshadowed by the gratitude he feels for Capone's good deed. Indeed, if Al Capone were a regular person who helped Natalie get into school, Moose would readily give him [or someone close to him] flowers. Once Moose realizes this, he knows he must try to grant Capone's request. Answers will vary.)*

5. After Annie refuses to play baseball, Moose comments that "Girls are impossible. Once they decide something, that's it. Guys make deals, make compromises, make things work. Girls just make trouble" (p. 62). Why do you think Moose made these comments, and what do they indicate about him? *(Answers will vary, but Moose's comments likely do not reflect any deep-seated beliefs. In this moment, he is upset with Annie for refusing to play. Also, note that Moose is just as stubborn as Annie by withholding what is going on with Capone. As such, there does not seem to be any logic to Moose's comment.)*

6. During Rocky's brush with death, the author uses italics and fully-capitalized words to make the scene more dramatic. Discuss the effect that the text's appearance has on how a story is read. Are text and layout important? Would you read the story the same way without the italics or fully-capitalized words? *(Answers will vary. You might retype this section of the story without any of the embellishments. Have students read your copy and then the one in the novel.)*

7. The civilians on Alcatraz form a small community. Moose is able to literally run Rocky to the doctor to save him. Would such a thing have been possible in a larger community or city? What are the pros and cons of living on a small, self-contained island such as Alcatraz? *(Answers will vary. Pros—Friends, essential goods, and medical attention are all within walking distance. Everyone knows each other, families spend a lot of time together, and in an emergency people work together to resolve a problem. Cons—It is hard to keep secrets, and dysfunctional relationships are especially problematic due to limited space and social options.)*

8. **Prediction:** Do you think Moose will be able to give the roses to Mae without getting in trouble? Explain.

Supplementary Activities

1. Figurative Language: Continue adding to your figurative language chart. Examples: **Similes**—"looks at me like he's expecting me to throw him a life preserver" (p. 40); "making them clatter like tiny galloping horses" (p. 41); "voice scratching like a match against flint" (p. 41); **Metaphor**—Natalie: octopus (p. 55)

2. Comprehension: Continue adding to your character chart.

3. Journal: In Chapter 5, the author describes Jimmy's and Theresa's living spaces. In a journal or personal notebook, answer the following questions: What do the children's living spaces say about their character? What does your own room say about your character?

4. Writing: Helen asks Moose to forgive her for not giving him enough attention. Write a poem about forgiveness from Moose's or Helen's point of view.

5. Health: Doc Ollie saves Rocky from choking on a penny. Research infant first aid for choking and CPR. How did these techniques originate? How are they administered? Find a brochure or pamphlet or interview the school nurse, and then create an informational poster about identifying and helping infant choking victims.

Chapters 9–15

Rocky recovers from the penny incident. Moose is shaken after Cam introduces him to Al Capone in the cell house hospital. Moose stresses about how he will manage to give Mae flowers. Piper is mad at Moose because he got to meet Al Capone. Jimmy tells Moose how important it is to him that Moose cares about the same things as him. Moose's parents encourage him to visit Natalie, and Moose agrees to go after realizing he might be able to share a ferry home with Mae Capone. He is also hopeful that Theresa, who is still upset about giving Rocky the penny, might agree to go with him. Theresa and Annie accompany Moose on his visit. Natalie is doing well and says that she is mad at Moose for not visiting her. Moose manages to give Mae a yellow rose by giving every woman on the ferry one.

Vocabulary
reliable
concealing
engage
elicits
disheveled
contingent
trellis
prompts
milling
rush
confers
flamenco

Discussion Questions

1. What happens when Moose meets Al Capone? How does the encounter make Moose feel? What might you have said or done in Moose's place? *(Al Capone tells Moose what a good job he has done and remarks that Moose seems like the kind of "person [who] keeps up his end of a deal" [p. 71]. While Moose's father is tough with Capone, Moose, starstruck and rattled, says, "Thank you." Fortunately for Moose, Cam does not understand why these words pop out of his mouth. Though Capone is friendly and calls Moose "son," Moose is unsettled by his interaction with Capone. He feels like Capone knows too much about him and his family, and Moose now knows without a doubt that Capone expects him to get Mae roses. Answers will vary.)*

2. In Chapter 10, Moose's father gives him advice about dealing with intelligent convicts who try to manipulate situations for their own gain. Why is this advice particularly significant for Moose? In what other scenarios might this advice be useful? *(Because Moose asked Capone for a favor that he granted, Moose is now indebted to him. He realizes that Capone is upping the ante, like*

his father says, by asking Moose to do something that poses an incredible amount of risk. He also realizes that now, the more he interacts in secret with Capone, the greater the power Capone has over him. This scenario is generally true whenever people share secrets. Secret agreements are only as safe as the people involved are trustworthy.)

3. Why is Piper mad at Moose? Is her anger justified? Why is Jimmy upset at Moose? Is his anger justified? *(Answers will vary. Piper is mad that Moose got to go into the cell house hospital and meet Al Capone. Piper had wanted to take Rocky to Doc Ollie since she gravitates toward any kind of excitement [Whether she really believed she was the fastest person for the job is debatable.]. She is very jealous of Moose's "reward." While Piper's disappointment is understandable, her anger at Moose is completely unjustified. The decision for Moose to carry Rocky was made in a split second by Jimmy [and to some degree, Theresa, who kept Piper from further complicating matters] at a moment when everyone was panicked and Rocky's life hung in the balance. In this moment, Piper's feelings were completely unimportant, so no one considered them. Moreover, no one could have predicted that the person who took Rocky would meet Al Capone. Jimmy feels Moose sometimes acts as if baseball is more important than their friendship. In addition, Jimmy is upset because he feels that he and Moose may not value the same things. Jimmy's feelings are understandable. Moose failed to defend Jimmy when Scout made fun of him and replaced him with Theresa. Moose tries his best to please Scout [for example, when he gives Scout his ball even though it is obvious he does not want to], yet he does nothing to show he cares about Jimmy's feelings during the game. Scout is a talented baseball player, and when he is around, Moose is most concerned with keeping him happy. Therefore, it is not hard to see why Jimmy believes Moose places a higher value on baseball than their friendship. Jimmy likes Moose and needs a close friend; it is natural that this incident would make him question if he really has a close friend in Moose.)*

4. Why is Moose hesitant to visit Natalie? *(Moose is worried that Natalie's school is not what he hoped it would be; in the past, he has found her schools depressing. Since he cares about Natalie and took a big risk to get Natalie into the school, he does not want to learn that it was not worth it. Further complicating matters are Moose's feelings of guilt. Moose knows it could easily have been him in the Marinoff School, had life dealt him a different hand. He feels bad that he was "lucky," and going to the school would only serve to remind him of that. In addition, in the short time since Natalie has been gone, Moose, for the first time in his life, has not had to think about anyone but himself and he has been enjoying a break from worrying about Natalie's needs. Lastly, Moose feels justified in not visiting since he has recently done something significant for Natalie. However, what Moose does not consider is that Natalie does not realize what Moose has done for her. She only knows that she has not seen him for some time and that she misses him.)*

5. Why is Theresa upset? Do you think Theresa should blame herself? How does Moose finally convince her to come out from under the covers? *(Theresa is upset because she gave Rocky the penny on which he choked. Answers will vary. Theresa is right to be shaken by the incident, but as Moose notes, it was also Theresa who made everyone aware that Rocky was choking and acted quickly so Rocky was saved. Also, Theresa is only seven and regardless of how Theresa sometimes feels about Rocky, the incident was an accident. She will certainly be more careful in the future. Theresa begins to stir when Moose says he sometimes wishes Natalie would go away. She comes out after Moose says not to listen to Piper's insults and alludes to his strained relationship with Piper. However, Moose's repeated attempts to make Theresa realize the unique ways she is valuable also probably encourage Theresa's emergence.)*

6. What surprises Moose when he visits Natalie? What do you think Natalie's life is like at her new school? Do you think it is a good place for her to be? Explain. *(Moose realizes how hard Natalie tries to communicate in conventional ways. She is really improving and is mad at him for not seeing her more often. Answers will vary. Encourage students to consider whether the school is treating Natalie with dignity and how her ability to express her feelings will affect her life. However lonely Natalie may be, the school is obviously helping her communicate better. Sadie may not understand everything about Natalie yet, but her firmness may be key in helping Natalie improve.)*

7. How does Moose manage to carry out his favor for Capone? Do you think Moose's decision to keep up his end of the deal is the right one? Explain. *(Moose tells the girls he is buying flowers for Piper. Later, he gives a flower to each of the women on the ferry so that giving one to Mae is not suspicious. He then tells the girls that he intended to give them flowers all along. Answers will vary, but since Capone is an unpredictable and powerful person, the Marinoff School is helping Natalie, and Moose felt indebted to Capone anyway, it does not seem an unreasonable course of action.)*

8. How do the various people who receive roses react to Moose's gesture? *(The women are all very happy to receive a rose. After some initial confusion, Annie is thrilled that Moose gave her a rose. Theresa remains suspicious, especially since she heard Mae address Moose by name. Bea, who more than likely feels underappreciated by Darby, proudly shows her rose to him and mentions her upcoming birthday. This causes Darby to have an even bigger grudge against Moose.)*

9. **Prediction:** Will Capone ask anything more of Moose? Explain.

Supplementary Activities

1. Figurative Language: Continue adding to your figurative language chart. Examples: **Similes**—"mad as a hornet" (p. 69); "has a fierce expression like she's chewing chain link" (p. 75); "bed…squeaks like a rusty bike" (p. 83); **Metaphors**—Theresa: lump (p. 84); Piper: second fiddle (p. 103); Natalie: loose cannon (p. 108)

2. Comprehension: Continue adding to your character chart.

3. Journal: Write a journal entry as Natalie expressing her feelings about her new school, her family, her friends, and her struggle to communicate with others. Include thoughts about how Natalie would like others to treat her.

Chapters 16–21

Darby questions Moose further about the roses, but Moose's answers are apparently satisfactory. Scout visits again, and Jimmy shows Scout the secret passage he has previously only shared with Moose. The island is preparing for a big dinner for J. Edgar Hoover and Eliot Ness, and Buddy Boy is working with Annie and Piper on a musical number. Moose's attempt to kiss Piper in the crawlspace is interrupted by Theresa. Mr. Mattaman and Mr. Flanagan both end up on probation after being falsely accused of drinking on duty. Natalie comes home and sets off the metal detector. Mr. Mattaman assumes one of her buttons set it off, but Moose discovers that she has smuggled in a bar spreader, which AZ 105 told her to put in her bottom drawer. Moose, Theresa, and Jimmy manage to get the bar spreader from her, and Jimmy sets out to throw it in the bay.

Vocabulary
lilting
gramophone
chiseled
residue
mortified
imbuing
vaudeville
specimen
simmer
wake
fib

Discussion Questions

1. Why does Annie ask Moose about whether he wants to get married and have children who play baseball? Does Moose seem to understand Annie's point? *(Annie really likes Moose, and she wants him to like her. She is trying to point out the advantages of being with her instead of Piper. Moose does not seem to understand that Annie is telling him she likes him.)*

2. Do you think Theresa really saw Mae Capone drop a handkerchief? If so, how might this be important? *(Answers will vary.)*

3. Why don't the other kids like to play with Janet Trixle? What do you think of Janet? How would you treat her if you lived on the island? *(Janet is known for bellowing into her bullhorn and being a stickler for rules. She likes to get her own way. Answers will vary. Students should note Janet's loneliness and willingness to help Moose in Chapter 17. Also, students should take into consideration that people, especially young people, are very often influenced by their parents' behavior. Janet's rigidity may not reflect who she truly is. These traits may be the result of a desire to emulate someone she naturally sees as a role model— her father.)*

4. Moose observes that Scout is "the guy who brings the eggs, but he's never the one with egg on his face. If he wasn't so much fun, I'd hate him" (p. 121). What do you think this means? Do you think Scout can be trusted? *(Moose notices that Scout causes trouble but never acknowledges or is held accountable for it. He insults Jimmy, yet Jimmy lets Scout in on a secret and Jimmy remains mad at Moose. He mocks Annie because she is a girl, yet after Annie proves her skills, all is forgiven. Answers will vary, but obviously Moose has his doubts. After Scout flirts with Piper in front of him for a second time, Moose gives Scout an ultimatum. Students should note that friendship requires a sense of loyalty to another person. Good friends consider how their actions affect others, and they are not opportunistic.)*

5. How does Moose react when Piper joins him in the crawlspace? Theresa thinks she saves Moose. What do you think? How does Piper react when Moose leaves to help Annie? *(Moose implicitly tells Piper he likes her by admitting that he was thinking about her and that he is jealous of Scout. Had Theresa not interrupted, he would have kissed Piper. Answers will vary. Piper is clearly upset that Moose leaves her.)*

6. Do you think Moose's and Jimmy's fathers were drunk on guard duty? If not, whom do you think got the two men in trouble? *(Answers will vary, but there is nothing to suggest that Cam and Riv are irresponsible. There is reason to suspect Piper since she is the warden's daughter and she is mad at Moose and Theresa.)*

7. What happens when Moose's parents leave the apartment for a few minutes after Natalie gets home? What do Moose, Theresa, and Jimmy decide they must do? What do you think of their decision? *(The children discover a bar spreader in Natalie's luggage. They are scared because Cam and Riv are already on probation. If the warden found out that a bar spreader made it onto the island, they could get fired. The children also realize that Natalie got the bar spreader from AZ 105, a former prisoner at Alcatraz who had shown romantic interest in Natalie. They decide to get rid of the bar spreader by throwing it in the bay, since convicts could discover it if they disposed of it in the garbage. When Moose's parents will not let him leave, Jimmy becomes responsible for the bar spreader's disposal. Answers will vary.)*

8. **Prediction:** What will happen when the person looking for the bar spreader cannot find it?

Supplementary Activities

1. Figurative Language: Continue adding to your figurative language chart. Examples: **Similes**—"The lilting sound of Mae's voice is spinning around like a gramophone inside my head" (p. 111); "Darby's face gets dark red like a kidney bean" (p. 112); "I'm like a gold digger the way I check everything…" (p. 117); **Metaphors**—Theresa's eyes: bowling balls (p. 115); kiss: ball of wax (p. 125); Moose: Humpty Dumpty (p. 127)

2. Comprehension: Continue adding to your character chart.

3. Journal: Write a journal entry from the point of view of Janet or Jimmy that discusses loneliness.

Chapters 22–26

Seven Fingers comes to the Flanagans' apartment to work on the plumbing, but Moose catches him looking for the bar spreader in Natalie's room. Moose tells his father he is worried about Natalie's safety at the school and that he thinks AZ 105 is visiting her, but Moose does not offer any real explanation for his worries. Natalie accompanies Moose to the warden's house, where she takes an interest in Willy One Arm's mouse. Moose talks to Piper about resolving the probation issue for Cam and Riv, and they kiss. Piper agrees to straighten things out on the condition that Moose helps her spy on Al Capone at the big dinner. Moose admits that he wishes Jimmy liked baseball, and Jimmy walks away disappointed and angry. Moose and Piper sneak around during the dinner, watching Capone in the kitchen and dining room.

Discussion Questions

1. Why is Moose worried that Seven Fingers is coming to fix the plumbing? Why does Moose tell his mother he is worried about being around Trixle? *(Moose believes it is no coincidence that right after Natalie's return there is something "wrong" with the plumbing. He thinks Seven Fingers will look for the bar spreader, and he is worried about what might happen when Seven Fingers does not find it. Moose lies to Helen so that she and Cam will not become suspicious and make Moose reveal his secrets.)*

Vocabulary
murmurs
quarantined
cocoon
transfixed
plumb
pell-mell
commandeered
oblivious
resounding
dapper
manipulates
podium
dour

2. What do you think of Moose's conversation with his father about Natalie's safety? Would you have taken the same approach if you were in Moose's place? Is it ever appropriate or justifiable to hide the truth? *(Answers will vary, but this is Moose's awkward attempt to protect both Natalie and his father's job. Moose does raise Cam's concern, though rather than commenting on what he knows, Moose still hides part of the truth by saying he became worried about Natalie due to a nightmare. As Moose stated earlier, if his father knew about the bar spreader, he would feel compelled to tell the warden about it and Cam and Riv would lose their jobs. Students may have different ideas about talking with Moose's father that would be more effective in communicating the potential danger, such as simply saying Natalie talked about AZ 105 visiting.)*

3. What conflicts occur at the warden's house? How are these conflicts resolved? *(At the warden's house, Piper does not want to talk to Moose and orders him to go away, Natalie does not want to give Molly back to Willy, and Moose must convince Piper to tell her father the truth about Cam and Riv. Piper eventually follows Moose outside and agrees to listen to him. Willy takes back his mouse, and Moose promises Natalie another visit to keep her calm. Moose agrees to owe Piper if she tells her father the truth, even though the whole mess is her fault.)*

4. What problem do Theresa, Jimmy, and Moose face after Jimmy gets rid of the bar spreader? What would you do in their place? *(Jimmy threw the bar spreader into the bay, but it washed up on shore. Janet has made it the centerpiece of her carousel, which is locked inside the Trixles' apartment. Answers will vary.)*

5. How does Jimmy react to Moose's honesty about his interest in baseball? Explain whether you think Jimmy's reaction is justified. *(Jimmy gets upset when Moose confesses that he wishes Jimmy liked baseball. Answers will vary. Looking at the situation through Jimmy's eyes, it is understandable that someone lonely like Jimmy might want his friend to be as similar to him as possible and that finding out that this friend is decidedly different might be upsetting. On the other hand, Moose has tried to take an interest in Jimmy's fly experiments; it does not seem like too much to ask that Jimmy show some interest in baseball. Moose is open-minded to Jimmy's interests not because he is a phony who is obsessed with everyone liking him, but because he genuinely likes Jimmy [regardless of their differences] and wants to interact with him in ways that interest them both.)*

6. What kind of person is Piper? What concerns might she have? Why do you think she blackmails Moose into staying at the dinner party with her? *(Answers will vary. Piper is someone who likes to get her own way and often seems to care little about the cost. Though* Al Capone Does My Shirts *showed that Piper could be manipulative, it is telling that Moose felt that jeopardizing Cam's and Riv's jobs would be out of character for Piper. The author has hinted that Piper's mother is ill, and with her father always being so busy, Piper may be feeling very scared and alone. Additionally, Piper knows there will be a new baby in the family soon and that if it is a boy, her father will be terribly proud. She may feel like she will cease to be important to him if a baby brother comes along. She likes Moose, as evidenced by the kiss on her front porch, and she wants him to be with her when she sees Capone so she does not have to sneak around by herself.)*

7. What can you tell about Warden Williams from the scene in which Hoover is pick-pocketed? What does the scene tell you about Piper? *(After Moose and Piper see Capone serve Ness and Hoover, Piper insists, "The show's not over" [p. 184]. That Piper knew this and that Warden Williams tells Hoover, "…it would be a bad idea to cut back our guard forces…" [p. 185] right after Hoover is pick-pocketed shows that Warden Williams orchestrated the entire incident. Though the warden did so for a good reason, the scene shows that he can be manipulative and sheds light on where Piper learned her manipulative ways.)*

8. **Prediction:** Will Moose and Piper get caught? Explain.

Supplementary Activities

1. Figurative Language: Continue adding to your figurative language chart. Examples: **Similes**—"A pelican dips and soars like a stunt plane" (p. 151); "…my legs feel like they are mortared to the couch cushion…" (p. 154); "My arms are stiff as sticks of wood" (p. 154); **Metaphors**—Seven Fingers: the picture of obedience (p. 152); Capone's face: the picture of submission (p. 183)

2. Comprehension: Continue adding to your character chart. If no new characters are introduced, consider whether there are facts about the current characters you can add to your chart.

3. Journal: Moose's father asks him, "Who are we to say what life's supposed to be about, Moose?" (p. 158). In your journal, write your ideas about what you think your life is supposed to be about. What are your goals and aspirations?

4. History: Research J. Edgar Hoover. Write a short biography of him that includes basic information as well as offices held and significant contributions he made to the United States during his government service. Also, create a time line that indicates significant events during his life.

Chapters 27–31

Moose and Piper make it safely back to the Mattamans' apartment, but they discover Natalie is missing. They find her at the warden's house, but not before Moose bursts through the back door and sees Piper's mother in a deathly state. Piper is very upset about her mother being so ill. The Mattamans discover the children's shenanigans when they return, and Moose, Theresa, and Jimmy must tell them about Piper's lie and their plan to set things right. Mrs. Williams is taken to the hospital, and Moose is sent to check on Piper and bring her to the Mattamans' apartment. The Mattamans forgive Piper for her lie, and Piper loses all control of her emotions, even apologizing for what she did to get Riv in trouble. The warden's wife begins her recovery from the difficult pregnancy while the warden, in a celebratory mood, returns to the island with his newborn son. Annie, Moose, Natalie, and Theresa comfort Piper at her home. Moose, Natalie, Piper, and her brother are ambushed by a stranger impersonating Jimmy.

Discussion Questions

1. What dilemma do Piper and Moose face when they first leave the party to go back to the Mattamans' apartment? How do they resolve the conflict? *(They realize they have not figured out how to get back without attracting the attention of the guard tower. Piper tells Moose that they must act like they are supposed to be there. They are able to convince Mr. Mattaman that they are just now getting home from Piper's performance.)*

Vocabulary
blasé
lashes
reluctantly
slate
concede
pulverizing
ushers
lapping
giddy
mimics

2. Why does Piper refuse to let Moose into her house when they are searching for Natalie? Why does Piper lash out at Moose and Natalie? Does this new knowledge about Piper's mother affect your opinion of Piper? *(Piper does not want anyone to see her mother so sick. Anyone who knows the pain her mother is in will by extension know the pain that Piper is in, and Piper does not like anyone to know that she is vulnerable. Moreover, seeing others' reactions to her mother's state can only make it harder for Piper to ignore the very real possibility of her mother's death. Piper screams, "Nothing is wrong!" and Moose observes, "...the louder she screams, the more she sees I don't believe her" [p. 192]. Piper is mad at Moose for inadvertently exposing her vulnerability and making her confront her anguish. In this scene it becomes clear that when Piper earlier told Moose, "My life is over" [p. 182], her comment was all too sincere. Between the threat of losing her father's love and her mother, Piper is overwhelmed and takes out her anger on Moose and Natalie. Answers will vary.)*

3. The children tell Mr. Mattaman the truth about why Moose and Piper came home late from the dinner the night before. Why do you think Mr. Mattaman does not want anyone else to know what happened? Do you agree or disagree with this decision? *(Mr. Mattaman does not like that the children took matters into their own hands, but he also realizes that Piper's lie is the original source and that Moose, Jimmy, and Theresa were collaborating to clear his and Cam's name. From his point of view, things have basically worked themselves out, so letting others know about the mess could only stir up trouble. Answers will vary.)*

4. Discuss Darby's conversation with Moose in the Flanagans' apartment. Why does Moose disagree with Darby? Based on Darby's comments, what kind of man is he? *(Trixle tells Moose that the Flanagans should put Natalie somewhere with other people like her and abandon her. He has a brother with a condition similar to Natalie's. His brother was sent away to live in a home, and Darby never visits. Darby believes cutting ties with "bad things" is important. Darby accuses Cam of being "too soft" to rid the family of Natalie. Moose believes that Natalie is valuable, and he wants to have her in his life. He believes that she deserves respect, even if her mind does not work the same way as most people's. Moose sees Natalie as a human being with dignity, and he knows she tries hard to connect with others. The scene reveals Darby Trixle to be a weak man incapable of dealing with complex emotions and reveals that his aversion to Natalie is really a symptom of unresolved issues with his brother's abandonment.)*

5. How do the children find out what is going on with Piper's mother? What else do the children learn from their eavesdropping? How do they react? *(Annie, Moose, Theresa, and Jimmy sneak into the crawlspace in Chinatown to listen to the conversation between Mrs. Caconi, Mrs. Trixle, Mrs. Mattaman, and Mrs. Bomini. They learn that Piper's mother is very ill and may not survive her pregnancy. They also learn that Piper is alone in the warden's house and that Moose will be asked to comfort her. The women also mention Annie's crush on Moose, which embarrasses Annie and surprises Moose.)*

6. What is significant about Piper's meeting with the Mattamans? *(Once Piper feels safe and forgiven in the Mattamans' apartment and feels the arms of a mother around her, Piper's fear of showing vulnerability is overtaken by her fear of her mother's death. As she receives love and grace from one of the families she has wronged, she feels remorse and apologizes for getting Mr. Mattaman in trouble.)*

7. Theresa does not want to accept Piper's apology, but her parents encourage her to do so. Do you think Piper deserves to be forgiven? Is forgiveness something people should always have to earn? Explain. *(Answers will vary. Note that Mr. and Mrs. Mattaman, out of their compassion for Piper, forgive her before she even comes to their apartment. They realize that she made a very bad decision, but they also see that at this difficult time Piper desperately needs someone to love her.)*

8. What kind of person does the warden seem to be? What do you think of his behavior after the delivery of his son? *(Answers will vary. The warden appears to be very self-centered. He brings the baby home before his wife is ready to leave the hospital and seems oddly unconcerned about his wife's well-being as she recovers. He seems to want to claim credit for his son's birth and does not mention that his wife's condition is improving.)*

9. The children find Piper in her room after the warden returns to the island with his son. How does Piper feel about her little brother? Why do you think Piper feels this way, and are Piper's feelings common? *(Piper does not like her little brother at all. She believes her father loves him more than he loves her, and she is mad that her mother almost died giving birth to the baby. Answers will vary. It is fairly common for children to fear being displaced when there is a new addition to the family, and Piper is still very stressed about all her mother has been through. Sometimes it takes time to connect to a new family member. It also makes sense that Piper would feel a deeper connection to her mother than to a baby she has only known for a day. Also, Piper's father has done nothing to ease her anxiety, involve Piper in her new brother's life, or properly introduce the siblings. He has only confirmed Piper's fears.)*

10. **Prediction:** Who is threatening Moose at the end of Chapter 31? What will happen to Moose, Natalie, Piper, and the baby?

Supplementary Activities
1. Figurative Language: Continue adding to your figurative language chart. Examples: **Similes**—"panting like they've just run a few miles" (p. 189); "head is like a little nodding machine" (p. 189); "skin as gray as dead fish" (p. 190); **Metaphors**—Moose and Piper: dead meat (p. 187); Annie: box with feet (p. 207); Walter: little turnip (p. 220)

2. Comprehension: Continue adding to your character chart.

3. Journal: Write a journal entry from Piper's point of view that sheds light on her complicated emotions and behavior.

Chapters 32–37

Buddy Boy, Willy One Arm, and Seven Fingers take Moose, Natalie, Piper, and her baby brother hostage. Willy One Arm leaves the baby at an undisclosed location, and the other kids are forced to accompany the convicts as they head down to the dock to make their escape. Natalie repeatedly indicates that the cons do not have guns, and Moose yells for help. Theresa, Annie, Jimmy, Janet, and numerous guards, including Cam, soon storm the scene. The cons are apprehended, Piper realizes she cares about her baby brother, and Natalie leads Moose and Cam to the cell house hospital, where they find Capone in his cell rocking the baby. It comes to light that Mae and Al Capone aided in the escape plan, and after days of questioning the guards, the warden realizes that blame for the fiasco must be shared by everyone, including himself. Al Capone sews a new button onto Natalie's yellow dress and leaves her a note that reads, "Good job."

Vocabulary

taut
agitated
adrenaline
obscured
clobbers
cleat
frantic
commotion
euphoria
envelops
evades
prosecuting
demoted
apprehend
emphatically

Discussion Questions

1. What catches the cons off-guard when they take the children hostage? What risks does Natalie and the baby's presence pose? *(They do not expect Natalie and the baby to be present and are only prepared to deal with Piper and Moose. Natalie could lose control of herself, and the cons would hurt her if she drew attention to them. The cons might also harm the baby if he begins crying uncontrollably.)*

2. As they are walking to the dock, how is Natalie key to foiling the convicts' plan? *(Natalie assures Moose that the cons do not have guns. Moose does not know for sure how she knows this, but he does know that Natalie is generally very accurate when it comes to counting things. This prompts Moose's cry for help, which sets in motion the chain of events that leads to the children's rescue and the convicts' capture.)*

3. How do the rest of the children help foil the convicts' escape? *(Jimmy's flies swarm the convicts as they head out on the boat. Annie pitches rocks at the cons, and Theresa and Janet run toward the boat, Janet calling for the cons to stop through her bullhorn. All of this activity slows down the cons and attracts many guards to the dock. In addition, when Buddy gets desperate, he comes out of the boat waving Mae's hummingbird hankie, erasing any doubts about Theresa's earlier observation.)*

4. Describe Cam's behavior when he arrives on the scene and rounds up the children. How would you feel if you were in his place? *(Cam is alarmed that his own two children were held captive by cons and that Moose is bleeding, but he is also proud of Moose's and Natalie's actions. He commands respect as an authoritative and reassuring presence in the midst of chaos. Answers may vary.)*

5. How did Seven Fingers escape? What happened to the warden's baby? How does Natalie know where to look? *(Seven Fingers escaped through the bars of the cell after cutting through them with dental floss and cleanser. It is the same hole through which Willy gave Al Capone the baby during the escape. Capone is found gently rocking the baby when the Flanagans arrive at the cell house hospital. Natalie finds the baby by following Willy's mouse to Al Capone's cell.)*

6. Capone claims he should not be punished since he was only taking care of the warden's baby during the escape attempt. Do you think Capone did anything for which he should be punished? Explain. *(Answers will vary, but Capone did quite a bit of harm. Though he did not attempt escape and took care of the warden's baby, he helped Seven Fingers by playing the banjo so he could not be heard sawing through the bars. He also had Mae intentionally drop her hankie, which contained the boat's keys, over the side of the ferry. Capone deliberately got behind in his shoe-shining so that Buddy and Seven Fingers would have guard shoes to wear during the break. Most glaringly, he did not alert the warden or the guards to the plan.)*

7. What does Cam mean when he says, "There's plenty of blame to go around" (p. 247)? How do you think the story would have been different if the children had told all they knew to the adults around them? *(The warden was distracted by his wife's failing health and then by the party he threw to celebrate his son's birth. The party collected all of the best guards, leaving the island vulnerable. In addition, the cons would have had a much harder time carrying out their plan if the warden had not allowed them so much freedom. The Flanagans did not tell others about AZ 105 or his contact with Natalie. The children did not tell anyone about the smuggled bar spreader, which Trixle did not even realize was in his home until Mr. Mattaman told him. No one noticed the sawing of the bars going on in Capone's cell. Answers will vary. Knowledge of the bar spreader [and perhaps also the missing handkerchief] could have helped those in charge realize the cons were up to something, but this would have come at the expense of Riv's and Cam's jobs.)*

8. What does Moose realize about the need for forgiveness? What does Moose learn about himself after what he has been through? *(Moose realizes that people do forgive each other, particularly when their offenses are put into a larger perspective. Answers will vary. Moose realizes that he does tend to try to please people. He sees that sometimes that tendency is harmless, as with Annie's mother, and that sometimes it can be problematic, as when he nearly went along with what the cons wanted him to do as they were heading to the boat.)*

9. Where does Natalie's new button come from? What do you think of the way the story ends? *(Natalie's new button is sewn on by Al Capone. Answers will vary.)*

Supplementary Activities

1. Figurative Language: Continue adding to your figurative language chart. Examples: **Similes**— "The fingers burn into me like a taut rope" (p. 225); "…his eyes are like points on barbed wire" (p. 226); "a sound like splitting wood" (p. 233)

2. Writing: The warden wants to keep the escape attempt secret to protect everyone who made mistakes leading up to the attempt. Pretend you are a journalist who catches wind of what happened. Write a headline and an article for the local paper. What is your story's headline? Which parts of the story will your article highlight? Remember to open the article with basic information about who, what, when, where, and why.

Post-reading Discussion Questions

1. Read the Author's Note at the end of the story. As a class, discuss which parts of the novel were based on truth and which were fiction. Did the story seem as though it could have been a real account? What are the pros and cons of reading a work of historical fiction? *(Answers will vary. Consider how historical fiction can pique someone's interest in historical events by bringing it to life in a way that nonfiction books often cannot. However, also consider that readers of historical fiction must take care to discern fact from fiction so they do not walk away with an inaccurate impression of historical events.)*

2. Throughout the story Moose receives both high praise and harsh criticism for his actions. What kind of person is he, and how does he change as the novel progresses? *(Moose has a quietly magnetic personality. One of the big problems that Moose, and indeed most of the characters in the story have, is that people immediately like him and want his attention. Moose, in turn, tries his best to be kind to everyone. In Jimmy's angriest moments, he would contend that Moose is nice to everyone because he wants to avoid conflict at all costs and needs to be loved by everyone. In Piper's angriest moments, she would contend that Moose is oblivious and dishonest. These accusations are largely unfair. It is true that Moose does not like conflict and that this partially explains his behavior toward others. However, time and time again throughout the story, it is obvious that however flawed Moose may be, he is usually primarily motivated by love, and luckily for those who know him, he has a lot to give. One example of Moose's genuine friendship and love comes when he is sent to comfort Theresa. Moose is not sure what to say at first and feels awkward, but he goes out of his way to make Theresa feel valued and even goes so far as to make a difficult admission to her—that like her, he has sometimes wished his sibling would go away. At the same time, Piper's assertion that Moose anticipates being rid of Natalie is untrue. Certainly, Moose and his parents enjoy a break from "the hubbub" that goes along with having Natalie around. However, Moose loves Natalie a great deal. He worries for her welfare at the Marinoff School, considers how it would feel to live with the challenges she faces, is upset that Natalie is angry with him when he visits, consistently treats her with warmth and dignity, and stands up for her whenever someone slights her, even if it means risking getting into trouble [as with the warden and Trixle]. Moose is also probably the only person capable of the patience, love, and sheer willpower necessary to endure Piper's volleys of emotional abuse and still comfort her. If Moose truly were selfish and superficial, he would not have committed himself to helping Piper. As for Jimmy, Moose cares about him, but Jimmy's loneliness demands more of Moose than he can possibly give. Jimmy might claim that Moose does not care about him because he is not really interested in his flies, but consider that Moose never makes a similar claim about Jimmy's disinterest in baseball. It is also worth noting that Moose is genuinely hurt and disappointed when Jimmy reveals their secret crawlspace to Scout and the other children. If in the past Moose has sometimes been too agreeable for his and others' own good, the incident at the dock where he nearly goes along with the cons' plan is disturbing enough to him that in the future he will likely curb his acquiescence.)*

3. Moose states, "Life is complicated. You'd think on a prison island—what with the bars and the rules and everything—it would all be so clear…but it's not" (p. 256). Which characters are the good guys, and which are the bad guys? What makes a person "good" or "bad"? Do some characters fill both roles? Explain. *(Answers will vary. Darby Trixle could be considered "bad" because he tries to create problems for the Flanagan family, such as when he blames Moose for the flat tire and has the tower fire shots to upset Natalie. On the other hand, he apprehends Seven Fingers during the prison break. Cam Flanagan seems an obvious choice for one of the good guys because of his tendency to look for the best in others and his unwavering integrity. Seven Fingers seems an easy choice for one of the bad guys since he is a convicted ax murderer who threatens*

Moose and Natalie and takes them hostage. Buddy Boy is harder to categorize since for much of the story he treats Piper kindly and Mrs. Williams with respect. However, he is obviously a skilled actor, and he does not seem to care about anyone during the escape attempt. Though he seems unwilling to kill the baby, he is complicit in the rest of Seven Fingers' plan. Al Capone, too, has some redeeming qualities but is ultimately more bad than good. He helped Natalie get into the Marinoff School and seems to respect Cam and his efforts to raise Moose right. He seems to only be kidding about employing Moose when he is released from prison, acknowledging that Moose is a "good boy" and remarking that he would be proud to have a son like him. Later Capone takes good care of the warden's son until Natalie, Moose, and Cam arrive. He tells Cam that Natalie is smart and congratulates her for her heroic efforts during the escape attempt with his "Good job" note and a new button. However, Capone is still someone who committed terrible crimes during his life, and he was key in facilitating the escape attempt. On the latter point, it is worth noting that he chose not to attempt escape himself, not because it would be wrong, but because he felt the escape plan was poorly conceived. Capone seems to be someone who, though he knows right from wrong and even admires some people who live good lives, is resigned to being one of the bad guys. He either feels he has far too much to atone for or believes himself incapable of dispelling the evil inside him.)

4. Cam Flanagan believes that the cons are not to be trusted. However, those that are trusted, like the passmen in the warden's house, are given more freedom. Do you think it is possible for a criminal to change his/her ways and function well in society? Do you think criminals usually return to their unlawful ways even after being punished? *(Answers will vary. Encourage students to support their opinions with logical claims rather than blanket statements. If appropriate, encourage students to research rehabilitation practices in some penitentiaries or even in local juvenile detention facilities.)*

5. Compare and contrast Darby Trixle and Cam Flanagan. *(Cam Flanagan believes that the cons should be treated as people although they cannot be trusted. Darby believes that cons should be treated like dogs, constantly kept on a leash, and treated poorly as punishment for their wrongdoing. They also disagree about how people who need help functioning in society should be treated. Darby believes those types of people should be sent to be with others like themselves and that families should abandon them because it is too painful to try to reconcile the two worlds. Cam believes his daughter is important and has unique and valuable gifts to offer the world, even if they often go unrecognized. He only wants her to go away to school so she can function better as part of the family and society. While the two men disagree about how people should treat each other, they do agree on issues of integrity. Darby is a stickler for rules, and Cam is unwavering in his choices to voice the truth and do what is right, even if doing so incurs undesirable consequences. Both men agree that the convicts are not to be trusted. Both are family men who care about their wives and children, even if the family dynamics are quite different.)*

6. Of all of Moose's friends, whom do you think is the best friend to him? To whom is he the best friend? *(Answers will vary, but Annie is probably Moose's best friend. Not only does he really enjoy playing baseball with her, but she always tries to give Moose good advice [even when it is not in her best interests, as when she tells Moose to get Piper red roses], and as Moose says, "She's nice. She's smart. I can trust her" [p. 192]. Moose is a good friend to a number of people, but Piper seems like a natural choice for the person to whom he is the best friend, if for no other reason than that she causes Moose more stress than anyone else he knows and yet he continues to be there for her when she needs him.)*

7. What are the effects of the following characters' self-serving behaviors: Warden Williams, Seven Fingers, Piper, Scout? *(Warden Williams throws a party in his son's honor and has all of his best men come to celebrate. As a result, security on the island is not as tight and three convicts take hostage four children—two of them the warden's own—and nearly escape. Seven Fingers tries to get the bar spreader from Natalie's room. He is discovered by Moose and frightens him by threatening Natalie's life. His escape plan jeopardizes Alcatraz's security and the lives of several children and guards. Piper is selfish in blackmailing Moose to stay with her at the banquet. As a result, Moose gets home later than expected and Natalie is missing. Scout is very self-centered and likes to play baseball, so if it seems that someone might impede his fun, such as someone who cannot play, like Jimmy, Scout does not mind insulting them. The incident drives a wedge between Jimmy and Moose that lasts the duration of the story because Moose fails to defend Jimmy.)*

8. How is it ironic that for much of the novel Piper and Theresa are at odds with each other? *(It is ironic because Piper and Theresa are actually quite similar in some ways. Both are stubborn, bratty, like being the focus of attention, and have trouble accepting new additions to their respective families.)*

9. Why do you think the author involved so many of the characters in the scene where the cons attempt to escape? *(The cons' attempted escape represents a major challenge for the non-criminal residents of Alcatraz. Most of the characters present have at some point in the story disappointed themselves and/or someone else. The cons' escape attempt is a high-stakes situation that tests everyone's character, giving them a chance to prove they are valuable or to redeem themselves. Cam proves to everyone that he is a reliable guard, and Moose proves that his primary motivation in life is not to choose the path of least resistance, but to do what is right. Darby's apprehension of Seven Fingers proves that he has heart, and Piper's strong desire to search for her brother shows that she can love him after all. Janet senses trouble when she spots Theresa running and grabs her bullhorn, which no doubt helps get the guards' attention. In this way, Theresa proves she is not a jinx but good luck and Janet proves she is a team player. Jimmy's flies and Annie's arm, both at different points slighted by Scout, are put to good use in deterring the cons' escape. Natalie, so often unfairly dismissed by others, emerges as perhaps the greatest hero, using her communication skills to alert Moose to the cons' lack of weapons and her intelligence to follow Molly to the baby. The scene reinforces one of the author's main messages in the story: "Nobody has all the pieces. We need each other" [p. 251].)*

10. By the end of the story, are all of the children's secrets revealed to their parents? If not, which secrets remain untold? What do you think would happen if these secrets were revealed? *(All of the secrets related to the breakout are revealed. However, Cam and Helen never find out about Moose and his friends' questionable behavior on the night of the big dinner for Hoover and Ness, and Moose still has not told any adults about his communications with Al Capone. Readers are reminded of the latter secret when Natalie gets a new button and her own note from Capone on the story's last page. Answers will vary.)*

11. Would you like to have lived as a civilian child on Alcatraz? Explain. *(Answers will vary.)*

Post-reading Extension Activities

Writing

1. Review the predictions you made while reading the novel. Choose one of your incorrect predictions. Write a new closing chapter that shows how the novel would have changed if your prediction had come true.

Art

2. Make a diorama of Alcatraz Island, labeling areas especially important to the novel.
3. Draw a caricature of Buddy Boy doing one of his impressions.

Drama

4. Develop a movie pitch for the novel. Suggest possible actors to play the major characters, and develop an outline suggesting how to tell the story.
5. Working with a small group, write and stage a scene from the novel. Add appropriate background music and lighting.

Social Studies

6. Mrs. Mattaman makes amazing cannolis. Find a recipe for cannolis, and attempt to make the dish yourself. (Note: Do not prepare food without adult assistance.)

Research

7. The novel says that Buddy Boy's talents could make him a star in a vaudeville troupe. Research vaudeville troupes of the mid-1930s. Create a poster advertisement about a troupe coming to visit a town. Include pictures and details about attractions and prices in the advertisement.
8. Rocky almost dies from choking on a penny. Research choking hazards, and create a pamphlet that informs people about which toys are safe for young children.
9. Moose, Scout, and Annie all enjoy playing baseball. Research famous baseball players, teams, and games from 1935. Write a report detailing what you learn, and create visual aids, such as baseball cards and posters, to display your findings.
10. Mrs. Caconi is very proud of her new icebox. Research the history of refrigeration. When did refrigerators as we know them become commonplace in the United States? When was air-conditioning, or "refrigerated air," first introduced? Write a report detailing your findings, and include some explanation of the science behind refrigeration.

Assessment for *Al Capone Shines My Shoes*

Assessment is an ongoing process. The following ten items can be completed during study of the novel. Once finished, the student and teacher will check the work. Points may be added to indicate the level of understanding.

Name _____ Date _____

Student **Teacher**

_____ _____ 1. Complete the Story Map found on page 27 of this guide.

_____ _____ 2. Complete the Characterization chart on page 28 of this guide for Moose, Darby Trixle, and Piper.

_____ _____ 3. Using at least ten vocabulary words, summarize a part of the story in which there is a conflict and explain how it is resolved.

_____ _____ 4. Prepare ten questions you would like to ask the author, Gennifer Choldenko. With a classmate, conduct a mock interview using these questions.

_____ _____ 5. Complete the Time Line on page 29 of this guide.

_____ _____ 6. Complete the Solving Problems graphic organizer on page 30 of this guide.

_____ _____ 7. Identify one theme in the novel. Explain the part it plays in the story and how it relates the author's message to readers.

_____ _____ 8. Write a short essay comparing and contrasting Moose with one of his friends.

_____ _____ 9. Complete at least two Post-reading Extension Activities, and present one to the class.

_____ _____ 10. Correct all quizzes taken over the novel.

Attribute Web

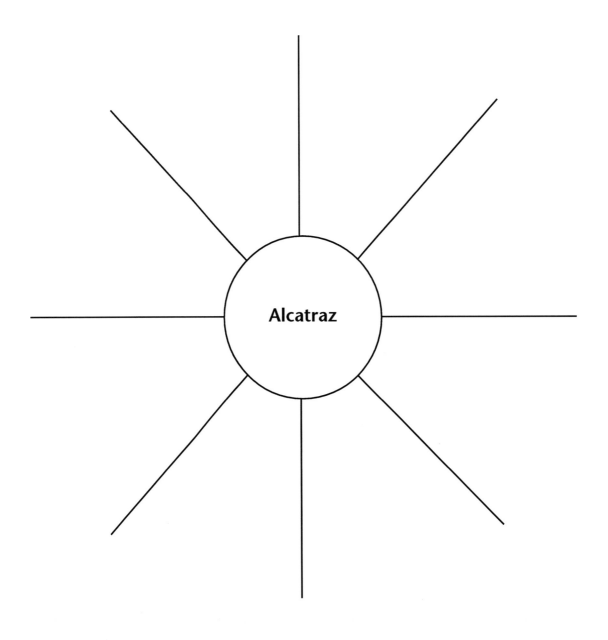

Story Map

Directions: Fill in each box below with information about the novel.

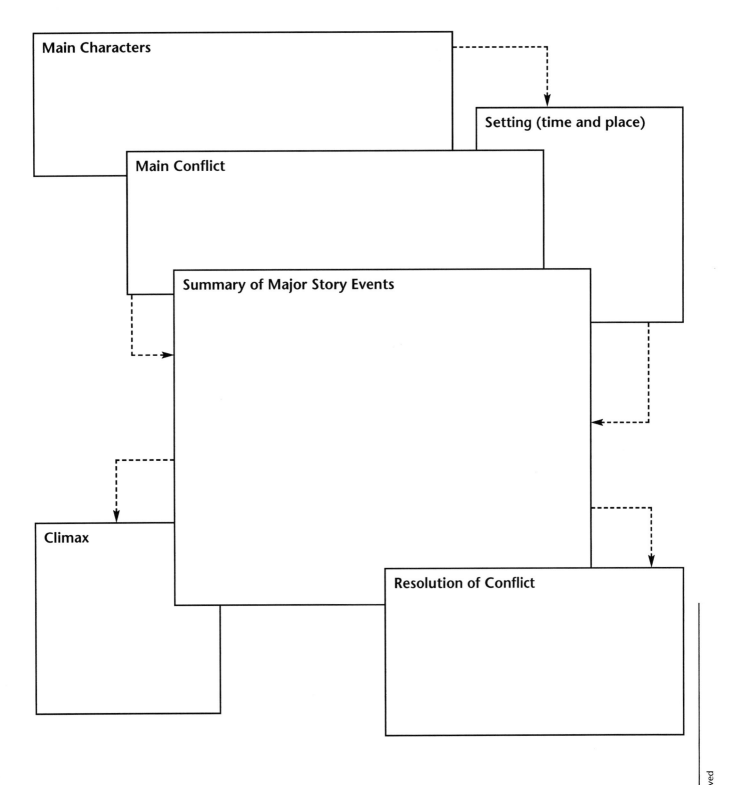

Characterization

Directions: Place the name of a main character in the center circle. Write a word or phrase describing the character in each oval. Describe a behavior (action demonstrating that trait) in each rectangle.

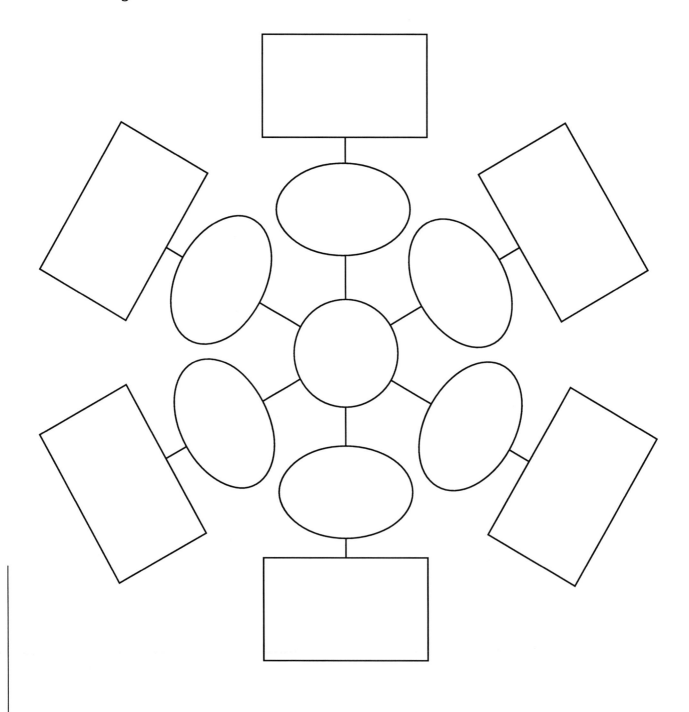

Time Line

Directions: In the numbered boxes below, write four main events from the novel in the order they happened. In the larger boxes, describe the event or draw a picture representing the event.

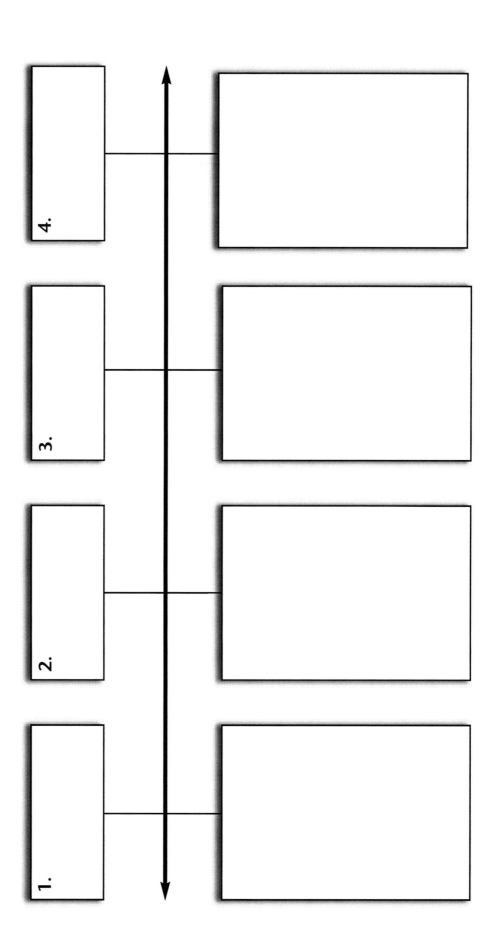

Solving Problems

Directions: List six problems the characters in the novel face. Then complete the rest of the chart. For each problem, circle which solution you think is best—yours or the character's.

Problem	Character's Solution	Your Solution

Linking Novel Units® Lessons to National and State Reading Assessments

During the past several years, an increasing number of students have faced some form of state-mandated competency testing in reading. Many states now administer state-developed assessments to measure the skills and knowledge emphasized in their particular reading curriculum. The discussion questions and post-reading questions in this Novel Units® Teacher Guide make excellent open-ended comprehension questions and may be used throughout the daily lessons as practice activities. The rubric below provides important information for evaluating responses to open-ended comprehension questions. Teachers may also use scoring rubrics provided for their own state's competency test.

Please note: The Novel Units® Student Packet contains optional open-ended questions in a format similar to many national and state reading assessments.

Scoring Rubric for Open-Ended Items

3-Exemplary	Thorough, complete ideas/information Clear organization throughout Logical reasoning/conclusions Thorough understanding of reading task Accurate, complete response
2-Sufficient	Many relevant ideas/pieces of information Clear organization throughout most of response Minor problems in logical reasoning/conclusions General understanding of reading task Generally accurate and complete response
1-Partially Sufficient	Minimally relevant ideas/information Obvious gaps in organization Obvious problems in logical reasoning/conclusions Minimal understanding of reading task Inaccuracies/incomplete response
0-Insufficient	Irrelevant ideas/information No coherent organization Major problems in logical reasoning/conclusions Little or no understanding of reading task Generally inaccurate/incomplete response

Notes